the stranger you are

the stranGeR
you are

Art by Gronk
Poetry by Gail Wronsky

TIA CHUCHA PRESS

ISBN: 978-1-882688-62-3

Book Design: Jane Brunette
Cover Art: "The Stranger You Are" by Gronk

PUBLISHED BY:
Tía Chucha Press
A project of Tía Chucha's Centro Cultural, Inc.
PO Box 328
San Fernando, CA 91341
tiachucha.org

DISTRIBUTED BY:
Northwestern University Press
Chicago Distribution Center
11030 South Langley Avenue
Chicago IL 60628

Tía Chucha's Centro Cultural & Bookstore is a 501 (c) (3) non-profit corporation funded in part over the years by the Arts for Justice Fund, National Endowment for the Arts, California Arts Council, Los Angeles County Arts Commission, Los Angeles Department of Cultural Affairs, The California Community Foundation, the Annenberg Foundation, the Weingart Foundation, the Lia Fund, National Association of Latino Arts and Culture, Ford Foundation, MetLife, Southwest Airlines, the Andy Warhol Foundation for the Visual Arts, the Thrill Hill Foundation, the Middleton Foundation, Center for Cultural Innovation, John Irvine Foundation, Not Just Us Foundation, Liberty Hill Foundation, the Attias Family Foundation, Life Comes From It, and the Guacamole Fund. Donations have also come from Bruce Springsteen, John Densmore of The Doors, Jackson Browne, Lou Adler, Richard Foos, Gary Stewart, Charles Wright, Adrienne Rich, Tom Hayden, Dave Marsh, Jack Kornfield, Jesus Trevino, David Sandoval, Gary Soto, Sandra Cisneros, Denise Chávez and John Randall of the Border Book Festival, Mountain Software, Luis & Trini Rodríguez, and other

 **contents**

Somos nosotros los que debemos ser adivinos.
It is we who must be the diviners.

Pharmakopoeia by Dale Pendell

A donkey will dig in dry mountain dirt
for a petrified potato. I'm a poet:

my divining rod pulls rubies
big as small boulders out of

the very same ditch. Rumi would say
the ruby and the potato are one.

Both are kissed by the abyss,

which every day we rise from,
looking out with alien eyes
at the stony face of a shining planet.

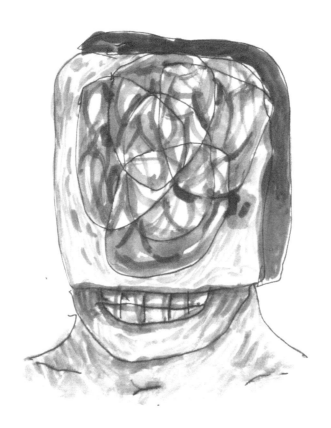

My brain is a museum of stones.

Even when we feel this way—like
jaded masonry—we are things through
which the stream of existence flows.

And yes, I've read the poems you left me.

You can tell that I like them—my
jade-gray teeth are glowing.

Even after I met you it was there—
like a giant Joshua tree made of rock.

All my sacred solitudes—
boulders held aloft by unshakable arms.

What am I but a mouse in the face of it?
What are you but a garden of mirages, too?

You took your daily dive into the lake
inside you. When you surfaced
you said, Nobody knows
who the dead are. That's the source
of their power over us.
Well, there you have it, I said.
Your eyes are like these stones, you said.
I found them in the caves at lake bottom.

I contain multitudes.
I am up to my eyeballs in personalities.

Now I've forgotten who I am.

Sometimes I think that my real face is the flipside
of the face I face out to the world.

In my dreams I have teeth,
in a world without other people.

You are aroused by the way I pose.

I'm just trying to be worthy of this ecstasy of roses.

Or is it a bowl of artificial fruit, cheerily dyed
For the cheap chapeaus of destiny?

How would I know?

I've been swimming all day in the water
in which embryos float.

My body the size of a toothbrush, more or less.

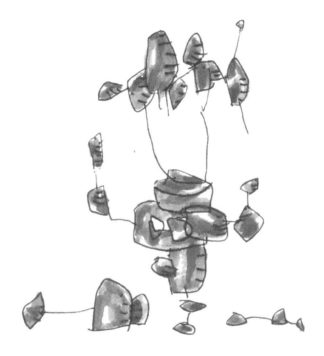

A teal light
softens it.
It has a certain level of
Zen seductiveness

and makes me remember

the way lotuses
exploded for us
back when it was all
Baby, please don't go.

You and I, wind, will lie down together
on this ball of barbed wire.
You flap
above me like a soft gray sheet.

I don't like the fact
that I'm mortal—
that I see the world askew
and hear the whispers of muffled voices.

I don't like the fact that
we go out like lights, while
somewhere yellow funeral flowers
smolder and creak.

The bodies were red
and vines among them rose greenly.

I sat in there for a long time
thinking of something I wanted to say to you—

something this side of intelligent—
something about how we're bodies, and that's that.

Wasn't the garden miraculous?
It had no fruit in it at all.
It had no death at all.

In serene irony the blue-green infinity

sprouted a giant claw that plucked me,

an inadequate poet, gutless, from the barren

wilderness of my sorrows. Now what?

It's kind of strange, isn't it?

All I can think about is you.

His face gave birth to red geometries.
He was subtracting
things from himself. This
was something significant and full of meaning

from an existential point of view. He used to devour
astrology and magic. He used to love poems.

What glow-in-the-dark Rubik's cube guided him
to this moment?
What wide knife just winged the day?

I was thinking of leaves
and feet (how they arch)
and necklaces.
There were commas and
semi-colons of light in my brain—
both inscrutable and excruciating.
I was really sad about the whole
perishing thing—how it makes
it all seems so ad hoc—
and then a leaf fell to my shoulder,
giving me the benefit of a
seasonal metaphor,
and time began again.
I saw the pain on your face
and thought of something positive
to say to you about this little moment
of uncertainty and grace.

And I know I won't write
squat. Maybe I'm nuts,
but I'm feeling as though
you and I, my muse, are
an urn made of two faces
that will never face
each other again—a red
drapery of glaze between us,
as bulletproof as rain.

In this theater of brutality,
even rocks look like profiles
of the newly dead.

The sky is full of their ghosts—
blue ghosts floating
all the way to the horizon.

Sometimes the afterlife
is all around you.
It creeps right up on you,
the way the titanium moon does
in daytime.

Sometimes it's all you're left with.

Often, I think of the person I
used to love, their thumb on my soul.

Once, when I gave them a wooden
match, they lit it with their teeth.

With you it's different: most days, we just
watch our shadows glide around us

as the sun goes by. We sit by still fountains
overgrown with moss. We're made of

wax. We've forgotten our names. Little
insects fly in and out of our mouths—

the first love and the second love,
they are not the same.

Hello, emptiness. My soul has
leapt right out of my brain. My
head, like a giant boulder, perches

on a cliff's edge wondering what
I'll do now for entertainment. The
dirt below me has sharp red fingernails

and a constant turbulent undertow of
moaning. I've forgotten the meaning
of the words *mother, seahorse, knife,* and

volcano. Maybe I'll rub my thumb across
my forehead, in effect rewriting my
face. Maybe I'll become a mirror

image of you. Do my metalloids
match, in any way, your anguish?
Please don't shoot me. Don't even

say the word *future.*

She had dwelt in the land of pain,
and everything was old to
her except for her oldness,

which was new. Red clouds billowed
behind her, behind her green hair—
its curls wound into tight green pearls.

My life, she said, *is, at the very least,*
something you could write an opera about.
if only someone else, I said, would,

as we roar toward death, write the music.

They tell me
I talk too much and write too little—

I forget to admire the sky—
that I see the truth only by

hearing. Last night, I was a girl
wearing a tutu that was also a mouth.

There was no green
moon to save me, only the stone-dark

gaze of a marble god who did
nothing to make things better. Inside the

whirl of dream I'm in tonight there are
red tsunamis; I'm desperate to find

the word *flesh* in a novel; I want
very badly to wash my face with the

wind. And for some other poet
to puzzle over all of it.

Bob Dylan smoked cigarettes. Wish I still could.
Wish I'd written a book called USEFUL INFORMATION
FOR THE SOON-TO-BE-BEHEADED. Wish I'd

written the phrase *like the blindness of noon.*
My mother wielded a mean sewing machine.
In my mind
I'm hanging on to a branch swept by wind.

My mind is like yours, no more
than a pot full of thoughts and sawdust!

Sometimes I'm the elephant in the room—
grazing pastures of ether while
people pretend not to notice
in the smoke of an autumn evening
my massive implacable grayness—
my beauty, rising from the underworld.

I live to fill books with awkward
meaning. And to
dance the dance of swans.

And the person inside me is frightened.
The flames
are vertical—two wavering spirits
standing upright in their graves.

The silence here
is like science—antiseptic.

And the person inside me is dying
to pat me on the back. I'm a poet—
this
is to be expected. If only
we had a pair of asbestos gloves.
If only we had arms.

I went as a man who one night
dreamt two dreams simultaneously.
Everyone laughed as I

held up the two selfies I took
while pretending to sleep.
I had thought about going as noise,

or as splattered gasoline,
as snow, as dust, as cinnamon,
as an oddly dressed puppet

made by a mad doll maker,
or as one of those ragged
Mongolian horses as swift as tigers.

Last year I went as a stream
of consciousness and got drunk
on myself. That, too, evidently,
was amusing.

You, reader, loom before me
like a golden statue—
the atom of my incarnation
in your eyes.

I'm dressed in Jesuitical black—
sexy—one drop of liquid
heroin behind each ear.

I'm trying to explain that I've
always relied on the kindness
of strangers. Your stoic
look is saying:
you haven't earned that phrase.

I hate those art-world clichés!

I'm tired of the endless battle to create
something new out of the void.

Perhaps I've already gone mad.
Is that why you're laughing?

Sometimes I think I'd like to rest
in a soft velvet case like a jewel.
And let that be the end of it.

As for poetry, I pray that it comes roaring
back into our lives like a steam rhinoceros.

We're powerless without it.

What are all these tall green things? you ask.
We call them trees.

A green claw has risen
like a puppet
from the end of my arm.

It is a beast that will feed me only
dry funeral cake.

It is a green beacon that beckons
lovers
and wants to pinch them too.

It's waving
to you like the sea, the green silk sea.

Sometimes I hide it under my shawl.
Sometimes it turns around and
scratches me. Sometimes

it grabs a pencil and writes,
Everything you
dream of can come true.

I am in love with it.

You failed to become poems.
You contained only a half-wisdom

buried in dream imagery and omens.
And just as I try to light you on fire

and toss you into the water, you
turn into origami blackbirds and

hover in the air in front of me. I
get it—it doesn't matter to anyone

whether you are good or bad—
I should have kept you. Now there's

only the dry sound of a lizard passing,
and off in the distance, someone

playing a shepherd's pipe.

Here I stand with my little scarf
which has one dot
like the bottom of a question mark
over my mouth.

Here's God's left eye
which has two white pupils.

Everything is slowing down.
Even the birds are flying more slowly.

And the dew of many deaths
rises to heaven like a candle-flame.

I used to be a woman of wisdom—
my thoughts as graceful as the swirls

of Pavlova.
Then I discovered the encyclopedia

of awkwardness. And the beauty of it
conquered me, taking all the oxygen

out of my philosophies.
Now, I spoon out peculiar

mouthfuls of poetry on tiny plates.
I call this life. Please, sit down.

Join me for a cup of bergamot.

Do you ever feel like you're standing
in a giant water glass
beneath a red cloud, complicated
as thought, and it's raining? I do.

Right down the road, two old women
are fighting each other like a pair
of angry lobsters. Did you know
that one of them is the person who
invented fire? I did.

So let's drink with pride the scarlet
rain of sunset in this paradise. It is ours.
We've earned it, having blood.

Well-disguised—in suit and tie—just
a half-eaten hors d'oeuvre the partygoers
overlook.

Sometimes I detach myself
from the fields and streets of walking pottery
so I won't be shattered into smithereens.

Sometimes I weep from one eye.

I am the self you never were—
the self you never knew how to be.
In human language, this is called love.
I also appear as a girl, or a puddle.

I'm hovering over a flame
and my body is made of ice.

In this predicament I realize,
one, I've made this fire

so my deep need for marvels
could be satiated—and

two, God made me ice
so that, ultimately,

I will be transformed.

Something bugs me.

Maybe it's this mantel around my neck.

Just when I've spent the day
charming publishers and muses (they
all want to be told that their eyes
are like deep-dark pools), those
red moths return,

hovering cynically around me. *So
what,* they say. *You write poetry. So what?*

To Hell with the power of the word, I say.

Some days you just want to make rice.

A love letter to my nightmare.

The person inside me
stroked their cheek with my chin
and thought about things.

Like the way all people are gods
with very short moments of incarnation.

Like the way no one
dances to the music
in my head even though it's
addictive—a red sound
verging on melancholy and ocher.

Lately I've been accommodating
myself to the cloud inside me.

It's whorl-like.
And inevitable.

It divides me.
Remember,

not too long ago, when everyone
was saying things were *perfect*?

Half of me does.

Why not a mannequin cut in half
at the waist and hiding
behind a broken tomato?

Why do all of our names begin with
I am and end with a torrent of lies?

Better to cover your face,
even though, as we all know,
you're still rather attractive.

Have you ever felt like
a steamship was headed for
your gullet? Well,

it is. So
let that velvet tongue of yours
unfurl. The sound you

utter will plunge
into people's ears like
an insidious hand grenade

and explode there quietly.
This will signal
that the hour of certain

ancient tragedies is arriving.
Welcome it
as if it were the wakening

of your most furious desires.
Remember that until this moment
you were lonely

and just about to cry.

Yes, I lifted the skull.
I said, *Alas, poor Yorick*.
But the skull in my hand
belonged to a monster.
Thoughts like gunshots
flickered all around us
in the communal graveyard.
The beastly skull said, *Why
the gloomy thinking, man?*
Everywhere, everywhere,
unspoken wisdom shed leaves
the way families shed lives.

I only want what's best for you.

Which is why I've got to say
that that giant blue ghost horse
you think you're standing under
isn't real. It isn't full of ghost
Greek soldiers. It won't help you
capture the famously beautiful
woman. Plus, even as an act of
the imagination, it's taking up a lot
of atmosphere in here.

And people are starting to talk.
Who's the guy with the giant blue
ghost horse that isn't real, they're
saying. It's you they're talking about—
you projecting your inner life
onto the world. You poet. It's you.

We touch the sky with our teeth—We stand
on enameled raindrops.
My ice cubes
help me steer through these dusky
rocks in search of meaning,
fleeting meaning. Why does it have to
mean something.

Pointed up, it scratches the sky.
Pointed down, it sends a shock wave
to the center of the earth
where our black roots were
entwined at the beginning.
It is an arrow. A divining rod.
My orange eyes watch you lift it.
What will you do now? Write
a poem? You are face to face with
the gods, wearing your last green
ball-gown. Do not disappoint me.

is the moment that awaits you.

Yes, you, with your three-part mind
and your hair cascading like blood.

We're just bodies, you say,
and that's that. I beg to differ, says

the person inside the person inside
your head—who isn't Bowie or Schopenhauer,

but hell, you listen anyway.

For Heaven's sake, in these uncertain
times take a seat in the hand
of God!
He's big and blue.
Three haloes of perfume
will crown you there. God will ask
whether or not you believe that the past dies,
to which you'll reply, yes, if the present cuts
its throat.

I pretended to be surprised when
blue ghosts fell
out of my laurel tree.

You can't let them know you knew they were
there all along.

You can't let them think you're not stunned
by their acrobatics. But you aren't.

You're simply waiting around
the way the dead wait, wondering when

you'll be crowned god of the lyric poem.

The day I came to the red cave
where poems are born,
wearing my best black dress,
you were inside, and we agreed
that although the exquisite glimmer
of eternity shines in the depth
of all suffering, we were tired
of the constant throbbing of police cars.
We were tired of the mass-produced
melancholy of these days.
We agreed that words that had once
been torn bleeding from our hearts
now seemed void of meaning.
May I come in? I asked. *Yes,* you said.
That word, as pure as a bird's song,
almost startled us both.

You're: an elegant hand holding up
a bouquet of black feathers.
I'm: a stick figure of a person
with flames on the top of my head.
I love you because you're flammable.
You love me because you haven't read
the warning labels. Someday, like all
good ideas, we'll be forgotten. But
meanwhile, we live here, on a planet
called Yesterday. It dies every night.

Don't fall off the giant
clown pants of life just because
you're having your picture taken!
See, right here I'm giving you the
benefit of a metaphor. It's
what I do—that, and warn people
not to talk shit about poets.

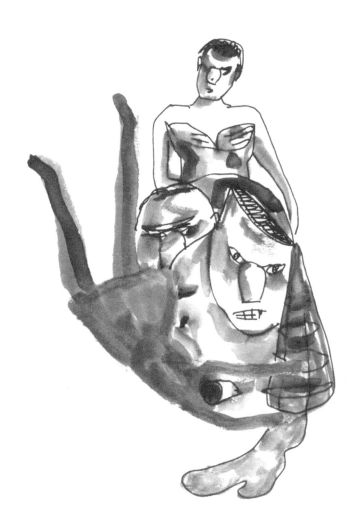

Do you remember my Marie Antoinette
incarnation? I wore ball gowns and ate

cake. Hungry red shadows flung themselves
at my feet. The faces of angry men peered

out from underneath my crinolines.
Life wasn't all that it was

cracked up to be. Now I live on the island
of bad movies with all the other dead

actresses. I've come here to tell you that
this poem you're looking at—it's a mirror.

They replaced your body
with an empty birdcage. And
gave me an empty birdcage
for a head. They gave
the woman next to us
a white robe with a cypress
tree on it, as if to say,
This is all there is—
emptiness and the color green.
But that was then and there. Not
here, on this page, where the
eye of the poet becomes the
great eye of light in the sky—
the thing the whole world turns
around. In a nightmare,
anything pointed can hurt you.
Anything empty is likely full
of inaudible sighing.

But maybe saying so means that I'm not.

It's just that instead of a head, a small
animal sits on my chest. In its mouth,
my left eye stares out crazily.
Let me feed it some blood.

She had no age.

She may have been
a hundred years
older or younger
when she stepped into
the spotlight,
raising her elk bone
scimitar operatically,
saying,
Remember, gentlemen,
I don't allow no table service
during my numbers.

Things like having a uterus
where my nose should be.
Like going to bed in a baseball cap
and waking up in a skirt.
Let's celebrate!
My mouth is a donut
and my very favorite poet has just
finished another wonderful poem.

Don't get me wrong—
there are worse things. I'll just
live among you, well disguised,
thanks very much. I'll wear a picture of your
face on my dress, the one made of red velvet
stage curtains, and walk in a garden of tall
wavering ghosts and green succulents with my
friend, a blue stinkbug. He's not Kafka's
cockroach, mind you. He doesn't say things
like, *we are the suicidal thoughts of God.*
He's simpler, more like, *let me go home
now and hug a Buddha.* I'm a simple
person. Simply trying to poeticize my way
out of all this disaster. Kafka's bug says,
Only the madman's lies are true.
(Sometimes he whispers in hyperbolic non-
sequiturs.) I say, *Maybe it's time to put some
duct tape on the saran wrap of our lives.*

To be one human being
is to be a legion of ghostly mannequins—

This morning mine are dressed
in suits of rosy
brown fur and red fish scales.

What is suffering but the death
of one of these creatures?

What is life but their chattering
between our night wounds
and our waking?

Where will we go today, my dears?
We have decided not to go anywhere.
The road, we say, *is coming our way.*

Night

speaks to itself in the syntax of night—
which sounds like the sacred wrinkling

of certain blue dresses, or like
the mechanical heartbeat of

submarines.
(There are never enough similes, I say.)

What an astonishing time we live in—
so full of science and

illumination—so, what's with all these
blue shapes coming toward me?

You rise from the cracked egg
of your birth holding an olive branch
out to the world. You are so tender
you think that a shadow falling on a piece
of paper might hurt it. But
the world you're given is a twisted
spiral of grids that your gaze can't
enter. What a savage joke this is.
Don't forgive anyone for it.

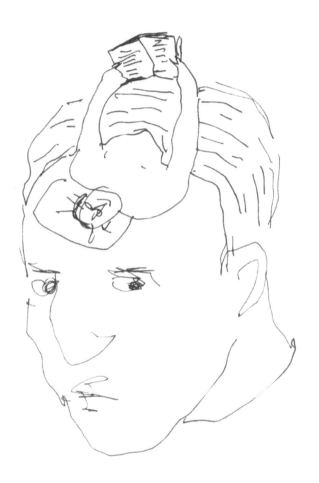

Marcel Proust wrote in bed.
The person inside my head
is reading Marcel Proust in bed.
Marcel Proust is saying that
poems are best when they aren't
saying anything at all. This is all I
have to say right now. That,
and this, that *too many things have*
perished which I imagined would last
forever. Which is precisely why
I like to look at pictures of birds—
they fly away. They take my sorrows
with them. It's like getting to be
alive all over again.

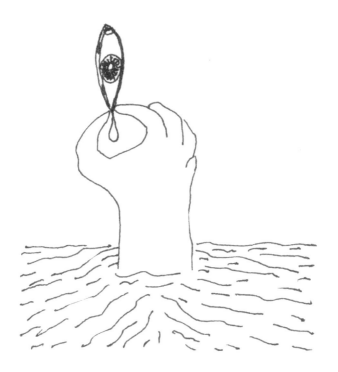

God was crying.
Her smile was frozen
somewhere in the northern sky.
One large tear fell like a hail stone
between my thumb and forefinger,
which I held up out of the ocean
like an OK sign.
Fairy tales at my age?
I swallowed the tear
because God knows that joy
is a wound we all must carry.
She is also a bird, and wind.
I was also drowning.

In this painting, at the end of a blue
vine, your ghostly blue body reaches
toward a gigantic pea pod full of fat
blue peas. Blue like the Danube

in moonlight emerging from a
subterranean spring. I'm hungry, I say,
as I begin my staring competition
with a sapphire leaf. If the true

problem of philosophy is what's for
dinner, from here it's looking like
blue pea soup for us, baby, blue pea
soup all the way down—

but where is the moon
in its nest of icy feathers?

Were you planning to skewer me?
It won't be the first time.

Do you remember, my love, those days
when we thundered together across the savannah?

Do you remember reading Baudelaire
as we languished in opium and poetry?

We were so simpatico.
We were hypnotized by our rapport.

Only your toothy smile can resuscitate
the otherwise dead soul of this: what
remains of me.

The rocket, years later, was to play
an important role in my life. That
and a blonde wig, not pictured here.

My hands were so cold I had to
warm them in your brain
with all the chicken corpses.

I'm just trying to say hello here
and you're walking away from me
with a blue divining rod in your hands.

You must be looking for the calmly
streaming waters of your childhood.

But last night
when we danced we moved like one
flame among many. We moved the way
blood moves beneath skin. We were
mad and admirable in our embracing.

Goodbye! Goodbye!
Don't die of fright tonight
when the sun sinks into my upturned palm.

Man holding plant: I think you're getting
dangerously nice.
Man who is a plant: Not true!
Man holding plant: I give you a lot of leeway for
your neuroses.
Man who is a plant: I can see the future and it's
sitting in the forest with the rest of us.

Are these our tombstones?

Are they magic doorways through
which we have to escape? If so,
I weigh less than the wing of a fly
and can't push anything open.

Are our nerves chattering like
parakeets in these cages?

The past, you said, releasing a smoky
breath, *one must wallow in it.*
Wallow in it. All the while
inventing what is new.

Have you finished the absinthe
I gave you, Picasso?

Maybe you can tell me what's
going on inside this shimmering.

Yes, you with the new blue antlers—
you doing a cartwheel off a cliff—
you with the head of a monster
breathing fire at your shoulder—

you holding a stick weighted like the
uneven scales of justice
(a brain on one end, a blood-drop
on the other)—don't

lay an expensive wreath on my
tombstone. Just put your fingers
there. Right there where blind pink worms
eat their way through my pretensions.

Then someone gave me this pet—
it has the red head of a monster
with pointy, jagged teeth.

When I take it for walks, people
run away screaming, even though
I try to convince them that he's
only dangerous when someone calls
him Ishmael.

My black dress scares them too.
It smells, incredibly, like the sea.

Here I am
striking out wordlessly across the skin
of the ground I walk on.

I'm off to find the flowery hillsides
of my childhood,

a pale gray sun hanging sullenly
ahead of me.

I'm leaving you and your gestures,
all duplicity and expectation.

I can see you without looking back.
Yes, you, exquisitely waving *adieu.*

Ever have one of those days?
My entrails were everywhere—

If my life were a sideshow
I would've walked on them

barefoot. I am the child of a
mandrake root. And I'm closing my

ears to the world, though I do love
its circularity.

Sometimes I forget that I'm not
on stage. Or, the opposite happens,
and the blood of the real

clots up the icy performances
of my nervous system. I remember
the time I said to you, in direst

sincerity, *May all the gods
of eternity and light watch over us.*
And you said, as you always did,

How about some vodka?
Were those just lines in a play?
Would you like a cup of coffee?

Its red steam is dancing like a bendy man
in front of the tragic blue mask
above my shoulders.

I'm just writing a book
with two characters in it:
God's eye and your Roman profile.
There's a lot of dramatic tension.
Who will win in the end?
I don't know yet, but your profile
is embroiled in a kind of inner
conflict. And God's eye is,
well, the eye of God. Your guess
is as good as mine. FYI, my writing
desk is a subterranean ocean. Oh,
and I have sharp teeth
like a crocodile.

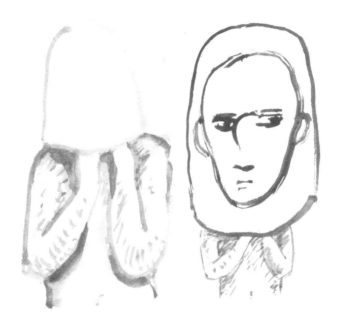

You're not a ghost, you're a block of ice.
And I'm having sad, bad memories tonight.

The way things stand between us now
I might not show you my slide show

of our past sexual encounters. Yes,
I am that petty.

And look where it got me.
I wanted to be a planet made of
diamonds.

Instead
I'm a lumpy sphere
made of really sad eyes
balanced precariously on
two ruined columns.

This is forever. And no one
calls me *my little blue marble* anymore.

In this drawing it looks
like your mouth is
a small cathedral, like I
could play the pipe organ
by pressing on your teeth . . .
Not in a time of quarantine,
of course, but after, when
I'm no longer wearing a
mask that has your face
drawn on it. Your eyes look
like the blue underwings of
a spotted moth from the family
Noctuidae. The word *Noctuidae*
makes me think of "A Night
in Tunisia," our favorite
Dizzie Gillespie tune.
That's why.

ACKNOWLEDGMENTS

Grateful acknowledgment to Jane Huffman and Diane Seuss for publishing the poems "It doesn't bode well, believe me" and "Why you aren't going to die" in *Guesthouse: A Panoply of Modern Writing,* Vol. 5, Summer 2020.

Grateful acknowledgment to the Bellarmine College of Liberal Arts at Loyola Marymount University for the Daum Professorship, which supported the writing of these poems.

Many thanks to Jane Brunette for her inspired and artful design, and to Luis J. Rodriguez for his commitment to the planet and its people, and for his belief in the transformative powers of poetry and art.

――――

That faraway, skirted creature in the beautiful painting: "cheap chapeaus of destiny" is an image taken from Rilke's *Duino Elegies.*

Final soliloquy of the beautiful lady in red: the last lines allude to William Carlos Williams' poem "The Last Words of my English Grandmother."

Everyone's writing a memoir: quoted lines are taken from Franz Kafka and Stanislaw Ignacy Witkiewicz.

Maybe we should just open a bottle of wine and watch TV: quoted line is from Marcel Proust's *Swann's Way.*